This book or parts thereof may not be reproduced in any form or by any means without written permission from the publisher, except brief passages for purpose of reviews.

The scriptures in this book are from different Bible translations.However, the "Encouragers" are the translation of the writer, Cheryl S. Weston.

Scripture quotations are taken from The Holy Bible New King James Translation (NKJV), Copyright@ 1982, The Life Application Bible New International Version (NIV), The Living Bible Copyright@ 1971, The Holy Bible King James Version Copyright @2005

Published by Grace Us Living Publications
Copyright © 2015 by Cheryl S. Weston,
All rights reserved.

ISBN 978-0-983218708

I0108919

Printed in the United States of America

TO KNOW HIM

Spending Time in His Presence

Devotional Journal

CHERYL SWINTON WESTON

Grow continually in the Lord, coming to know Him more and more each day. Grow in knowing Him in the power of His resurrection (the demonstration of everyday miracles signs and wonders) and in the fellowship of His suffering (trials, tribulation, problems, issues, service, love and sacrifice unto Him. (Philippians 3:10)

This Journal Belongs to:

_____

_____

_____
Date

Dedication

To all who want to know Him
more intimately...

Acknowledgments

To God, ALL Glory to You!

To my children, El/Tameika, Natasha and Trisha
To Ganny heart strings, Jamyre, Jaydyn, Tyler, Eliana,
I love you much, much, much, too many muches to
say...

To Momma, thank you for loving me; especially
during times when I was unlovable...

To Rebecca (Bec), thanks for being the walking,
talking example of "unconditional love" ... I love you.

To the women in The Power of Praying Women
Ministry, keep travailing in prayer!

To Reverend Daniel Simmons, thank you for
believing in me. Your persistence of reminding me to
"write that paper" helpedin discovering my gift as a
scribe.

To Apostle Sammy C. Smith, thank you for your
spiritual impartation.

To Pastor Michael Hamilton & his beautiful and
anointed queen, Suzette, thank you for your
provocative & profound love, care, wisdom and
prayers!

To every challenge, trial, and tribulation, thanks for
helping me to grow...

I surrender ALL...

Prayer

Father, thank you for your love, kindness and faithfulness towards me!

As I begin my journey of spending time alone with you, my desire isto get to know you more intimately.

Please, forgive me for all of my sins and trespasses. Help me to forgive others. Cleanse me from all unrighteousness.

Open up my understanding. Pleasehelp me to identify with your revelations, while I talk, listen, read and meditate on each scripture.

Please give me the desire to pray always, while Your Word transform my mind and heart.

Draw me closer to you. My desire is to be a emulate and become a reflection of You!

Thank You Father. In Jesus name, AMEN

My Covenant

I am committed

To set time aside

"To Get Know Him"

In Jesus Name

Name

_____

Table of Contents

Introduction

"To Know Him" was written after experiencing several very intense spiritual seasons. God has done a miraculous spiritual stretching or revival in me. It is true that to grow into a more intimate relationship with God, you must experience your own personal revival. While in your spiritual stretching, it's difficult to recognize the transformation taking place. It's when you arrive to the other side, you can recognize the transformation. The reality was God calling me to a more intimate relationship with Him.

There is a spiritual embryo in all of us. Seeking God for answers to life's problems and issues is a spiritual journey that each person has to go on or process through. In order to stay on course and give birth to your destiny, you cannot allow your everyday trials and tribulations distract or stop you from growing and developing spiritually. In fact, it's the uncomfortable seasons that will push you into spending more personal time with God.

Ultimately, God's desire is for His creations to get "To Know Him". He created man to worship Him, but we must emulate and become His image. I could remember times in my life, I went through some of the most painful, unfamiliar, uncomfortable seasons; and I was angry at God. As I searched for answers to many "whys" and unanswered questions, I didn't realize my search was actually leading me to a more intimate relationship with God. Issues of abandonment, betrayals, disappointments and traumas, pushed me into discovering who I was and who He was by getting "To Know Him". During the uncomfortable seasons, while reading the scripture, talking to Him and simply spending time with Him God was loving, consoling affirming and approving me. He was preparing me for greater things ahead by strengthening me to endure anything and by sharpening the tools of my gifts.

"To Know Him" Devotional Journal will encourage and help you to spend more time alone with God. Each chapter includes scripture guided "Journeys" that will inspire you to seek Him in your daily life. Within each "Journey" you will find an "Encourager", Scripture and a few lines to journal your "Heart Notes".   The journal ends with a Confession/ Prayer. As you speak the Word of God out into the atmosphere, your faith is ignited as your confessions manifest.

There is evidence of great men and women of God throughout scriptures that were persistent in seeking God to know Him. Even with your busy schedule, if your desire is to know Him, intimately, you too must put a demand on God. Set aside a little of time, and begin declaring, "God I want to know You and, the power of Your resurrection."

I pray that "To Know Him" will bless your life!

Come
To
Me

Journey One

Come To Me

Encourager

God is calling you to spend some intimate time
with Him! He loves you so much and is waiting
for you to bring every one of your concerns to
Him. When you surrender your heart to him, and
set time aside daily to spend with Him, you will
discover His Love for you. He knows your
hidden desire of knowing Him intimately. His
desire is that you experience the true meaning of
the power of His resurrection. Cast your care
upon Him. He is waiting to hear your concerns
and lift your heavy burden. There is no situation
too hard for Him. It doesn't matter where you
came from, what you've done or what you are
faced with, God loves you so much. He is calling
you to Him!

Scripture

Matthew 11:28-30
*Come to me, all who labor and are heavy laden, and I
will give you rest. Take my yoke upon you and learn
from Me, For I am gentle and lowly in heart, and you
will find rest in your souls. For my yoke is easy and
My burden is light. (NKJV)*

Come To Me
Heart Notes

_____

_____

_____

_____

_____

_____

_____

_____

_____

_____

_____

_____

_____

_____

Come To Me

Encourager

The future of Paul's followers was so important
to him, praying andtravailing in the spirit for
them became a way of life for him. As a mother
travails in birth, you too must travail through
your most painful and difficult times. Your
promised future will not come to pass if you
don't travail. God knows about your mistakes,
life's issues and struggles. No matter how great
the pain or who caused the pain, ask God to help
you through them and forgive others. He willgive
you clear understanding about the purpose He
have for your life. He will help you, and be with
you through all of your heartache and pain.
Actually, He will use the pain to strengthen and
shape you into becoming more Christ like.

Scripture

 Galatians 4:19
*My little children, of whom I travail in birth again
until Christ be formed in you, (NKJV)*

Come To Me
Heart Notes

_____

_____

_____

_____

_____

_____

_____

_____

_____

_____

_____

_____

_____

Come To Me

Encourager

As long as you live, you will go through problems, trials and tribulations. The feelings you experience from them, never feel good. In fact, the pain sometimes so uncomfortable and unbearable, you think that you won't be able to make it through. Drawing near toGod will help you during your most difficult time. God inspired anointed men to write the bible for us to read, especially during the most difficult times. Reading, meditation of the Word and praying are the painkillers needed lift the burden and heal the pain. The more you mediate on the Word of God, faith is increased; and your soul and spirit is healed. God's Word is the medicine and the guide that will lead you in your daily life.

Scripture

Psalm 1:2
But his delight is in the law of the Lord, and in his law he meditates day and night. (NKJV)

Come To Me
Heart Notes

_____

_____

_____

_____

_____

_____

_____

_____

_____

_____

_____

_____

_____

_____

_____

Come To Me

Encourager

God created you in His likeness and His image.Spending quiet time with Him is for the purpose of becoming more like Him. His plan is that you know the power He placed in you. God desire is for you to rule, dominate and operate, so you can carry out your individual assignment on earth. Time spent in His presence will help you to discover your purpose. It is necessary that you make a conscious decision of reserving specific times to be with Him. God does realize the busyness of your daily schedule, but you need Him to team up with you to bring your vision to pass. Invite Him with you on your journey. As you follow Him, you will look like Him.

Scripture

Genesis 1: 26
The God said, "Let us make man in His image, in His likeness (NKJV)

Come To Me
Heart Notes

_____

_____

_____

_____

_____

_____

_____

_____

_____

_____

_____

_____

_____

_____

Come To Me

Encourager

The bible clearly advises us that we should seek first the Kingdom of God and all other things will be added. As you submit yourself to God, your passion for the things of God will increase. Sometimes it is a battle to stay committed to prayer and the reading of God's Word. You simply don't *'feel'* like it sometimes. Regardless to what your flesh feels like, asks the Holy Spirit to strengthen you in your prayer time. Stay committed in your pursuit of Him. Search for Him and allow the ways of God to build your spirit with strength. God's Word will give you understanding of knowing what His Will is for your life. Therefore, you will be less tempted to be led away from God and your committed time alone with Him.

Scripture

Psalm 119:1-5
Blessed are they whose ways are blameless, who walk according to the law of the Lord. Blessed are they who keep his statues and seek Him with all their heart. (NKJV)

Come To Me
Heart Notes

_____

_____

_____

_____

_____

_____

_____

_____

_____

_____

_____

_____

_____

_____

Come To Me

Encourager

Jesus is not referring to a physical hunger, but of righteousness. Sometimes it takes desperation for answers that causes a hunger for God. He is your source and is the only ONE that can make the necessary resources that you need. Your persistence in seeking Him, will keep you focus, devoted and committed, to your time in God's presence. We sometimes allow "things" to distract us, and God's desire is for you to have some of life's finest things. Keep in mind that nothing physical can take the place of God's presence. In fact, some material things only give instant gratification; and cannot replace what your spirit longs for Him. When you feed your heart with God's Word, it fills your heart, mind, and spirit with ever lasting peace and contentment.

Scripture

Luke 6:21
My heart and my soul hungers for the Lord: and therefore, I am filled. (NKJV)

Come To Me
Heart Notes

_____

_____

_____

_____

_____

_____

_____

_____

_____

_____

_____

_____

_____

_____

Come To Me

Encourager

Jesus confronts Simon about the depth of his love for Him. If God was to ask you about your love for him, can you answer Him honestly? God's love is so deep,wide, pure and unconditional for you. He loves you to the point that He will maneuver the entire universe just to reveal His Love. Whatever, your needs are, He knows, and have your answer. The questions to you, how much will you maneuver your life to express your love for Him?

Scripture

John 21:15
So when they had dined, Jesus saith to Simon Peter, Simon, son of Jonas, lovest thou me more than these?(KJV)

Come To Me
Heart Notes

_____

_____

_____

_____

_____

_____

_____

_____

_____

_____

_____

_____

_____

Get
To
Know Him

Journey Two

Get to Know Him

Encourager

The solidity and strength of your spiritual foundation is based on accepting and getting to know God personally. It's when you confess that you need Jesus to lead and guide your life. Believing in your heart that God gave His Son, Jesus for you,and as you read the Word of God. It will penetrate your heart. God will strengthen, build your faith and produce strong muscles that will enable you to go through any process.

Scripture

Romans 10:9-10
That if you confess with your mouth, "Jesus is Lord," and believe in your heart that God raised him from the dead, you will be saved. For it is with your heart that you believe and are justified, and it is with your mouth that you confess and are saved. (NKJV)

Get to Know Him
Heart Notes

_____

_____

_____

_____

_____

_____

_____

_____

_____

_____

_____

_____

_____

Get to Know Him

Encourager

It is almost impossible for humans never to get anxious. You probably are no different. You worry about yourself, family members, careers, school, finances, and many other things. In this scripture, Paul advises not to be anxious, but turn your worries into prayers. An example of this is every time you feel like you are getting anxious, stop and pray. Realizing God's peace is always with you. He knows everything you are going through. His peace guards you with calmness, protection, and reassurance. The flesh wants you to worry and stress, and eventually, give up and quit. God's has given you peace and rest, while journeying through whatever you are experiencing, always thankful!

Scripture

Philippians 4:6-7
Do not be anxious about anything, but in everything, by prayer and petition, with thanksgiving, present your requests to God. And the peace of God will guard your hearts and your minds in Christ Jesus (NKJV)

Get to Know Him
Heart Notes

_____

_____

_____

_____

_____

_____

_____

_____

_____

_____

_____

_____

_____

Get to Know Him

Encourager

Prayer is simply talking to God. God is your Loving Father and He is always there for you. He is concern about your needs, but also wants to have a close and intimate relationship with you. He is the Loving Father who should be honored as being holy. He loves it when you take the time to talk with Him. He cares about what is going on in your life and is interested in what you have to say. He wants to hear about your doubts, fears and insecurities, as well as your needs, and desires.

Scripture

Matthew6:9
This is how you should pray: "Our Father In Heaven Hallow be Your name. (NKJV)

Get to Know Him
Heart Notes

_____

_____

_____

_____

_____

_____

_____

_____

_____

_____

_____

_____

_____

Get to Know Him

Encourager

Jesus gave this prayer as a model for praying. Traditionally, these scriptures have been named, Our Father's Prayer". Itteaches and guide what you are to pray for daily. As you pray, God will meet your needs and your faith will grow. You are to pray to God but because Jesus makes intercessions for us through the Father, therefore, you must end your prayers, "In Jesus Name". This model prayers help you to talk to God about the areas in your life that need His attention.

Scripture

Matthew 6:9-13
Our Father in heaven, Hallowed be your name, Your kingdom come, Your will be done, On earth as it is in heaven. Give us today our daily bread. Forgive our debts, As we also have forgiven our debtors, And lead us not into temptation, But deliver us from the evil one."(NKJV)

Get to Know Him
Heart Notes

_____

_____

_____

_____

_____

_____

_____

_____

_____

_____

_____

_____

_____

Get to Know Him

Encourager

Knowing the Word and prayer are both your spiritual weapon you can use against anything that tries to abort or cancel God's assignment on your life. Daily fellowship in the Word, prayer and praise and worship is your survival kit. Spiritual hearing reveals what God is saying. It's not an outward loud hearing, but a hearing in your heart. You can discern what good, evil, truth and what is false. Discernment is your searchlight in identifying what is TRUTH. Therefore, you are led by the Holy Spirit and not false prophets.

Scripture

I John 4:1
Beloved, do not believe every spirit, but test the spirits, whether they are of God: because they are many false prophets have gone out into the world. (NKJV)

Get to Know Him
Heart Notes

_____

_____

_____

_____

_____

_____

_____

_____

_____

_____

_____

_____

_____

Forgetting
The
Past

Journey Three

Forgetting the Past

Encourager

There are many past experiences that could be used as testimonies of encouragement. The Bible gives many examples of faithful men and women. They endured and were victorious over their struggles, trials, and tribulation. Their testimonies encourage and reassure that you too can win the race of life. If they went through difficult times and came out victorious, you can too. The bible gives us the examples, so when you get weary, you draw the strength needed to move on. Strength is produced through hard trials. The longer you run your race, the greater your chances of jumping over hurdles to get to the finish line. Stay in the race and don't give up!

Scripture

Hebrews 12:1
Therefore we also, since we are surrounded by so great cloud of witnesses, let us lay aside every weight, and the sin which so easily ensnares us, and let us run with endurance the race that is set before us. (NKJV)

Forgetting the Past
Heart Notes

_____

_____

_____

_____

_____

_____

_____

_____

_____

_____

_____

_____

_____

Forgetting the Past

Encourager

You cannot go into your future without letting go of unhealed and unresolved issues of your past. God can then move you into your next phase of life. Whatever wound that is in your past, don't allow the pain from it, cripple or place your life on hold. Surrender it to God. Walk away from it. Put it behind you. Ask God to heal you, There is nothing that God can't heal. You may not feel healed, but don't let how you feel determine your healing. You gave it to God, leave it with Him. God has given you the ability to soar like an eagle. Unresolved past issues will keep you on the ground. Don't let your wound hinder you from soaring. Just as God was in your past, He is in both your present and in your future.

Scripture

Philippians 3:13
Brethren, I do not count myself to have apprehended; But one thing I do, forgetting those things which are behind and reaching forward to those things which are ahead. (NKJV)

Forgetting the Past
Heart Notes

_____

_____

_____

_____

_____

_____

_____

_____

_____

_____

_____

_____

Forgetting the Past

Encourager

No matter what your past look like, asking God for forgiveness is an open door to a bright and prosperous future. You have the freedom to boldly petition Him in prayer. In the Old Testament days only the high priest could enter into the holy room and petition God. In the New Testament, Jesus came and gave you the privilege to go before Him boldly. Jesus death and His resurrection removed all prayer restriction. Now you can go into God's presence, any time for any reason.

Scripture

Hebrew 10:19-20
Therefore brethren, having boldness to enter the Holiest by the blood of Jesus, By a new and living way which He consecrated for us, through the veil, that is, His flesh (NKJV)

Forgetting the Past
Heart Notes

_____

_____

_____

_____

_____

_____

_____

_____

_____

_____

_____

_____

_____

_____

Forgetting the Past

Encourager

There are many negative feelings that develop through deceptions. Denial, shame, low self-esteem, blame, pride, hopelessness, and abandonment are just a few. As you journey through these deceptions, forgiveness, prayer and God's Word will free you from these negative deceptions. In fact, conquering these deceptions can develop, mature and qualify you to help others. Journeying through the deceptions and coming out victorious is what actually empowers you for God to work through you! God can do far more than any negative deceptions or your carnal mind can think of, comprehend, guess or even imagine!

Scripture

Ephesians 3:20
Now to Him who is able to do exceedingly, abundantly above all that we ask or think, according to the power that works in us. (NKJV)

Forgetting the Past
Heart Notes

_____

_____

_____

_____

_____

_____

_____

_____

_____

_____

_____

_____

_____

_____

Forgetting the Past

Encourager

Jesus uses *"the"* in relation to Himself being truth. He didn't say He was *"a"* truth. He said he was *"the"* truth. The reality of getting to know Him is permitting Him to be the only teacher. Every other voice must submit to His voice and every other so-called truth must bow its knee to Him. Therefore, if you haven't accepted Him as Lordship, you must be willing to submit to what He teaches, you may consider telling Him this. "Lord Jesus, I am a sinner, please come into my heart, live in me. Lead, guide and direct my life. I believe you die and was resurrected for me. Thank You for saving me. Now you are a believer if you weren't before! Praise Him. Forget the past. You can move forward!

Scripture

John 14:6
I am the way, the truth and the life. No one comes to the Father but through me. (NKJV)

Forgetting the Past
Heart Notes

_____

_____

_____

_____

_____

_____

_____

_____

_____

_____

_____

_____

_____

_____

_____

Forgetting the Past

Encourager

Be careful of allowing negative experiences to hinder your spiritual growth and development. In fact, suffering is the great manure that could help your growth. The more trials and tribulation you experience, the power those things had on you, releases you. They no longer affect you. Therefore, you no longer sweat the "small stuff". God wants your primary focus to be in getting to know more about Him.

Scripture

Philippians 3:8
Yet indeed I also count all things loss for the excellence of the knowledge of Christ Jesus my Lord, for whom I have suffered the loss of all things, and count them as rubbish, that I may gain Christ. (NKJV)

Forgetting the Past
Heart Notes

Forgetting the Past

Encourager

Fellowshipping with God will remove your old ways of thinking, speaking and doing things. Negative things you speak will produce negative behavior. Good character is not necessarily taught, but it can be caught. Getting rid of old negative speaking and behavior, positions you into newness. Spending time alone with him will renew, transform, and empower you to be a doer of the Word.

Scripture

Colossians 3:8-10
But now you yourselves are to put off all these: anger, wrath, malice, blasphemy, filthy language out of your mouth. Do not lie to one another, since you have put on the new man who is renewed in knowledge according to the image of Him who created Him.(NKJ

Forgetting the Past
Heart Notes

_____

_____

_____

_____

_____

_____

_____

_____

_____

_____

_____

_____

Forgetting the Past

Encourager

Ask God to remove all sorrow and negative feelings from past grief. Grief is something that everyone experience from time to time, but you do not have to journey the path of grief alone. He can free you from entertaining your thoughts, feelings and emotions.God's Word and prayer is the map you need to get you to your next place in life. Though family and friends can offer support, only God Word can lead you into His path and into the light of your spiritual destiny.

Scripture

Isaiah 42:16
I will bring the blind by a way they did not know; I will lead them in paths they have not known. I will make darkness light before them.
(NKJV)

Forgetting the Past
Heart Notes

_____

_____

_____

_____

_____

_____

_____

_____

_____

_____

_____

_____

_____

_____

The
Power
of
Forgiveness

Journey Four

The Power of Forgiveness

Encourager

There is a supernatural power that is unleashed when you release the spirit of forgiveness. The negative effect and power of unforgiveness is the energy that energizes bitterness and resentment. Therefore, forgiving, free you from the grips of Satan's power and connect you to God's power.

Scripture

Matthew 5:44
But I tell you: love your enemies and pray for those who persecute you. (NKJV)

The Power of Forgiveness
Heart Notes

_____

_____

_____

_____

_____

_____

_____

_____

_____

_____

_____

_____

_____

The Power of Forgiveness

Encourager

The world believes that one should love those who love them, but Jesus requires that you love and forgive those who have caused you hurt, pain and sorrow. In fact, it is the people that have caused you the most pain, that have the greatest need for your love. It is sometimes hard to forgive but deliverance and power is unleashed and released when you forgive. Give away that unconditional LOVE. God gave it to you!

Scripture

Matthew 5:43
You have heard that it was said, Love your neighbor" and hate your enemies.' But I tell you: Love your enemies and pray for those who persecute you.(NKJV)

The Power of Forgiveness
Heart Notes

_____

_____

_____

_____

_____

_____

_____

_____

_____

_____

_____

_____

_____

The Power of Forgiveness

Encourager

Jesus uses the example of measuring grain in a basket to ensure the full amount. When you criticize others instead of showing love and compassion, the same measure will be done to you. If you give love and have compassion, the same will be return to you. The same quantities and qualities, in which you give, will be received. We are to love others, not judge others. You reap what you sow!

Scripture

Luke 6:38
Give and it will be given to you: Good measure, pressed down, shaken together and running over, will be poured into your lap. For with the measure you use, it will be measured to you. (NKJV)

The Power of Forgiveness
Heart Notes

_____

_____

_____

_____

_____

_____

_____

_____

_____

_____

_____

_____

_____

_____

_____

The Power of Forgiveness

Encourager

Forgiving requires that your feelings of anger, rage, and resentment must be released through the deliverance and healing power of God. The truth is, it is okay to get angry. Anger is a part of God's original plan. But you are not to remain angry. Whatever your reasons for being angry, go ahead and be angry, but get over it, quickly. Never use anger as a fuel for revenge because it will lead to tiredness, bitterness and resentfulness.

Scripture

Ephesians 4:26
Be angry, and do not sin. Do not let the sun go down on your wrath. (NKJV)

The Power of Forgiveness
Heart Notes

_____

_____

_____

_____

_____

_____

_____

_____

_____

_____

_____

_____

_____

_____

_____

The Power of Forgiveness

Encourager

Forgiving others is important to your freedom in Christ. In fact, your spiritual growth process is on hold until you learn to forgive. If you do not forgive others, God will not forgive you.

Scripture

Matthew 6:14
For if you forgive men when they sin against you, your heavenly Father will also forgive you.(NKJV)

The Power of Forgiveness
Heart Notes

_____

_____

_____

_____

_____

_____

_____

_____

_____

_____

_____

_____

Healing Scars
of
the Soul

Journey Five

Healing Scars of the Soul

Encourager

Jesus is the door for all of your need. Acknowledging your hurt and pain is the beginning of your healing. Not letting go of hurt, hinders your spiritual growth. I agree, you cannot forget your past feeling of pain, but God's love can open the door to your heart, so He can heal you. He may be knocking! Let Him in. His love will heal and strengthen you to move on. Leave the negative effects of the traumas of pain behind. Use your past pain, only as a stepping stone into your future. He is waiting for you to ask "God heal the inner scars of my soul."

Scripture

Revelation 3:20
Behold, I stand at the door and knock, If anyone hears my voice and opens the door, I will come in to him and dine with him, and he with me, (NKJV)

Healing Scars of the Soul
Heart Notes

_____

_____

_____

_____

_____

_____

_____

_____

_____

_____

_____

_____

_____

_____

Healing Scars of the Soul

Encourager

Emotional and mental wounds are the scars of one's soul. Because we live in an imperfect world, it's impossible to live life without pain. Everyone experience hurt and pain to varying degrees, but you can avoid allowing the pain toremain in your soul. Ask God to purge your heart, reveal and remove all unclean and evil that's in your soul. When you deposit God's Word in your soul, heart, and body, you are growing spiritually. Therefore, all the hurt and pain that have been deposited in your soul is in the process of becoming HEALED in Jesus Name!

Scripture

James 1:21-22
Therefore lay aside all filthiness and overflow of wickedness, and receive with meekness the implanted word, which is able to save your souls. But be doers of the word, and not hearers only, deceiving yourselves. (NKJV)

Healing Scars of the Soul
Heart Notes

_____

_____

_____

_____

_____

_____

_____

_____

_____

_____

_____

_____

_____

Healing Scars of the Soul

Encourager

You often put more emphasis on what you see with your natural eyes. What you see when you look in the mirror is usually not the picture of what is in the soul. Our soul stores our feelings and emotions. Many of life's hurt and pain causes trauma to your soul. The soul cannot be seen with the natural eye, therefore, when you look in the mirror, you only see a natural sight. The mirror can not reveal the reflection of your soul, only God's Word can. As you look in the mirror, use the Word of God to call those things that is not out of your soul and let the Word of God enter and bring healing. Your soul will then look like the image you want to see in the mirror.

Scripture

James 1: 23-24
For if anyone is a hearer of the word and not a doer, he is like a man observing his natural face in a mirror; For he observes himself, goes away, and immediately forgets what kind of man he was.(NKJV)

Healing Scars of the Soul
Heart Notes

_____

_____

_____

_____

_____

_____

_____

_____

_____

_____

_____

_____

_____

Healing Scars of the Soul

Encourager

Jesus know what's in your heart and soul. He wants to heal you. He won't force an entry into a wounded heart and soul. All doors of the heart must open from the inside and the pain must be released by you. For you to open these doors, you have to trust the Lord and be willing to walk through your issues with Him. He is waiting to heal your heart and soul.

Scripture

Revelation 3:20
Behold, I stand at the door and knock. If anyone hears My voice and open the door, I will come in to him and dine with him, and he with me (NKJV)

Healing Scars of the Soul
Heart Notes

_____

_____

_____

_____

_____

_____

_____

_____

_____

_____

_____

_____

_____

Healing Scars of the Soul

Encourager

When we go to the Lord with an honest and open heart, He can do anything. Even during times when God does miraculous healings, He often healsthrough a process. This process teaches how to live your lives healed. You can trust Him never to do anything in your life that will harm you. The devil wants you to believe that God is disgusted with you and is far removed up in heaven somewhere, far away from your hurts. That's not true.The Bible reveals the opposite.

Scripture

Matthew 12:20-21
A bruised reed he will not break, And smoking flax he will not quench, Till he sends forth justice to victory; And in his name gentiles will trust. (NKJV)

Accepting
The
Truth

Journey Six

Accepting the Truth

Encourager

One of the first things we must understand in order to know God intimately is accepting His Truth. Only the truth has the power to make us truly free. This freedom comes when you submit the wrong thinking and beliefs, and submit it to God's truth.

Scripture

John 8:32
And you shall know the Truth, and the truth shall make you free. (NKJV)

Accepting the Truth
Heart Notes

_____

_____

_____

_____

_____

_____

_____

_____

_____

_____

_____

_____

_____

Accepting the Truth

Encourager

A wrong perception builds itself around the stronghold of pride. Jesus couldn't minister to the arrogant and deceived Pharisees. They had a number of bondages that needed to be broken which was passed on for several generations. However, they refused their healing because they rejected the truth of Jesus. When you can admit that you need Jesus, you will then receive freedom.

Scripture

John 14: 6
Jesus said to him, "I am the way, the truth, and the life. No one comes to the Father except through Me."(NKJV)

Accepting the Truth
Heart Notes

_____

_____

_____

_____

_____

_____

_____

_____

_____

_____

_____

_____

_____

Accepting the Truth

Encourager

Asking the Holy Spirit to teach you the truth about God is vital. The best way to learn about God is to be taught by God Himself. The Holy Spirit is God. He has been sent as the third person of the Godhead to minister truth to you. He takes the things of God and personally ministers them to those who submit their heart and mind. As you learn about God, you need the leadership of the Holy Spirit. It is impossible to lie or distort the truth. The result is transforming.

Scripture

John 116:13-15
However, when He, the Spirit of truth has come. He will guide you into all truth; for he will not speak on His own authority, but whatever he hears he will speak; and He will tell you things to come.

Accepting the Truth
Heart Notes

_____

_____

_____

_____

_____

_____

_____

_____

_____

_____

_____

_____

_____

Accepting the Truth

Encourager

You can rests assure knowing that God has fulfilled every promise. His truth says you are blessed. Your situation in the natural may look like you are not. Truth before time seems like a lie. If God said it, it will happen! Every Word that God has spoken will come to pass. God is with us just as He was with Moses and our fathers. Start praising Him in advance for whatever you believe God is doing in your life.

Scripture

1 Kings 8:56
"Praise be to the LORD, who has given rest to his people Israel just as he promised. Not one word has failed of all the good promises he gave through his servant Moses. (KJV)

Accepting the Truth
Heart Notes

_____

_____

_____

_____

_____

_____

_____

_____

_____

_____

_____

_____

Accepting the Truth

Encourager

Speaking kind words is like giving away honey. When we speak kind words to others, they soothe, heal and produce a warm, loving and healthy environment. The sweetness of the confession of God's Word over and over, heals the body, soul and mind and encourages others.

Scripture

Proverbs 16:24
Pleasant words are like a honeycomb; sweetness to the soul and health to the bones.(NKJV)

Accepting the Truth
Heart Notes

_____

_____

_____

_____

_____

_____

_____

_____

_____

_____

_____

_____

_____

Accepting the Truth

Encourager

What an awesome guide the Holy Spirit is! When
you submit your minds to the Holy Spirit and the
Word of God, you can be healed of every
impediment that hinders your understanding of
God. One of the greatest challenges for someone
with a distorted image of God is to learn and
think of Him in new ways.

Scripture

John 16:13
*However, when He, the Spirit of truth; for He will
guide you into all truth; for He will not speak on His
own authority, but whatever he hears; He will speak;
and He will tell you things to come. (NKJ)*

Accepting the Truth
Heart Notes

_____

_____

_____

_____

_____

_____

_____

_____

_____

_____

_____

_____

_____

_____

Stay Free
In
Jesus Name

Journey Seven

Stay Free In Jesus Name

Encourager

Praying early in the morning is the best time of day. It is during this time, your mind is free from any worry or concerns. Therefore, you can commit your day to God and He will guide you throughout your day. Whatever time of the day you use as your morning, use that time as your praying time!

Scripture

Psalm 5: 3
My voice You shall hear in the morning, O Lord; In the morning I will direct it to You. (NKJV)

Stay Free In Jesus Name
Heart Notes

_____

_____

_____

_____

_____

_____

_____

_____

_____

_____

_____

_____

Stay Free In Jesus Name

Encourager

When you begin your day in worship, He draws nearby cleansing your heart. Listen and acknowledge when the Holy Spirit speaks. The Holy Spirit will sometimes reveal things about you that you may not want to hear. Listen and take action! It is may be hard on your feelings to turn away from actions that you may have been engage in for a long time. Your freedom lies in your obedience. Trust Him; He is directing your path for your daily and future journey!

Scripture

James 4:8
Draw near to God and He will draw near to you. Cleanse your hands, you sinners; and purify your hearts, you double minded. (NKJV)

Stay Free In Jesus Name
Heart Notes

_____

_____

_____

_____

_____

_____

_____

_____

_____

_____

_____

_____

_____

_____

Stay Free In Jesus Name

Encourager

God supplies all of your needs and deserves all the praises you can give Him. Having a heart of gratitude shows Him how much you appreciate his Love for you. Praising God frees you from all the things that are difficult and uncomfortable in your life. God inhabit your praises!

Scripture

I Chronicles 16:25a
For the Lord is great and greatly to be praised; (NKJV)

Stay Free In Jesus Name
Heart Notes

_____

_____

_____

_____

_____

_____

_____

_____

_____

_____

_____

_____

_____

_____

Stay Free In Jesus Name

Encourager

In spite of your imperfections and sins, God is in love with you. When you confess your sins and receive Jesus Christ as Lord, your relationship began. Once you received Jesus in your heart, there are three important disciplines you need to establish your life. These disciplines will keep your relationship with Christ real, fresh, and growing. They are praying, reading the bible and yielding to the Holy Spirit. God's gift of Grace will always cover you in your imperfections.

Scripture

Ephesians 2:8-9
For by grace are ye saved through faith; and that not of yourselves; it is the gift of God: Not of works, lest any man should boast. (KJV)

Stay Free In Jesus Name
Heart Notes

_____

_____

_____

_____

_____

_____

_____

_____

_____

_____

_____

_____

_____

_____

_____

Gift
Connection

Journey Eight

Gift Connection

Encourager

If you have not figured it out by now, everything you have been through in life has been ordered by God. No, God didn't cause them, but He allowed the enemy or gave him permission. God does have a plan for your life. You had to go through the processes of the good, the bad, and the ugly times. It was those experiences that has made you an expert and has qualified you to enter into the purpose God have for your life.

Scripture

Jeremiah 29:11
For I know the thoughts that I think towards you, says the Lord, thoughts of peace and not of evil, to give you a future and a hope. (NKJV)

Gift Connection
Heart Notes

_____

_____

_____

_____

_____

_____

_____

_____

_____

_____

_____

_____

_____

Gift Connection

Encourager

The fruit of the Spirit areattributes which grows naturally out of the spirit. It is character builders that empower you to love and serve others with Christ-like characteristics. God often uses the trials and tribulations of life to develop and mature the fruit. Notice I said fruit, not fruits. The nine is a bunch or group that must be developed in order to connect you with others the way God intended.

Scripture

Galatians 5:22-23
But the fruit of the Spirit is love, joy, peace, longsuffering, kindness, goodness, faithfulness, gentleness, self-control, Against such there is no law. (NKJV)

Gift Connection
Heart Notes

_____

_____

_____

_____

_____

_____

_____

_____

_____

_____

_____

_____

_____

Gift Connection

Encourager

Sometimes you may question what God is saying to you. During those times, keep seeking. Just as your natural father would give you whatever you ask. God the Father does even more. Everything you have asked God for is already released in the spirit. You must pull it out of the spirit through prayer of the Word. Persistent prayers unlock the door to the answers you need.

Scripture

Matthew 7: 7-11
Ask, and it will be given to you; seek and you will find, knock and it will be opened to you. For everyone who asks receive, and he who seeks find, and to him who knocks it will be opened. Or what man is there among you who, it his son asks for bread, will give him a stone?
Or if he asks for a fish, will he give him a serpent? If you then, being evil, know how to give good gifts to your children, how much more will your Father who is in heaven give good things to those who ask Him!(NKJV)

Gift Connection
Heart Notes

_____

_____

_____

_____

_____

_____

_____

_____

_____

_____

_____

_____

Gift Connection

Encourager

Once you have developed an intimate relationship with your Loving Father, you can serve others with a sense of contentment, joy and peace. Your heart is glad. How you serve others, shows how you serve God. Serving God with gladness means it doesn't matter where you are or what you are doing, you are just happy to be connected to Him. Therefore, your joy will be evident and your life is full of blessing Him.

Scripture

Psalm 100:2
Serve the Lord with gladness. (NKJV)

Gift Connection
Heart Note

_____

_____

_____

_____

_____

_____

_____

_____

_____

_____

_____

_____

Praise
&
Worship

Journey Eight

Praise & Worship

Encourager

You must always praise God. He inhabits your praises. He expects you to praise Him. God is not like man, He is King who sacrificed His Son, Jesus for you. Could you do that? He is the only wise God and He deserves the honor and glory forever. God is great, not just because of what he does in your life, but because of whom He is. What a glorious and marvelous thought!

Scripture

1Timothy 1:17
Now to the King eternal, immortal, invisible, to God who alone is wise, be honor and glory forever and ever.(NKJV)

Praise & Worship
Heart Notes

_____

_____

_____

_____

_____

_____

_____

_____

_____

_____

_____

_____

_____

Praise & Worship

Encourager

No matter what goes on in your life from day to day, praise and worship God for everything. Praise Him for being with you in ever thing that you go through. Praise Him for the strength, character and integrity that will be produce through your trial and tribulations. Know that weeping may endure for a night, but joy comes in the morning. Praise and worship Him for some of the hell you have gone through. Your life will become a lifestyle of praise and worship.

Scripture

1Timothy 1:17
Praise, honor and glory be unto the King who is eternal, immortal, and invisible. He is the only wise God and He deserves the honor and glory forever and ever. (NKJV)

Praise & Worship
Heart Notes

_____

_____

_____

_____

_____

_____

_____

_____

_____

_____

_____

_____

_____

_____

Praise & Worship

Encourager

Telling the Lord how you feel about Him is how you express your love for Him. It is good to say it out aloud. It allows you to hear yourself adore Him. The bible says faith cometh by hearing and hearing the Word of God. When you hear the Word, it builds your confidence and increases your faith. You will mature to the point that you will want to praise and worship the Lord with all your heart, soul, and all your strength.

Scripture

Deuteronomy 6:5
You shall love the Lord with all your heart, with all your soul, and with all your strength. (NKJV)

Praise & Worship
Heart Notes

_____

_____

_____

_____

_____

_____

_____

_____

_____

_____

_____

_____

_____

_____

Praise & Worship

Encourager

You dwell with God because you are in need of
His guidance. He is also your source of strength.
Dwell is a place of how you think, write or speak.
Dwelling with God is the safest place for you.
God's goodness and mercy will always lead,
guide and protect you day by day and
throughout your entire life.

Scripture

Psalms 23:6
*Surely goodness and mercy shallfollow me all the days
of my life; and I will dwell in the house of the Lord
Forever (NKJV)*

Praise & Worship
Heart Notes

_____

_____

_____

_____

_____

_____

_____

_____

_____

_____

_____

_____

_____

Praise and Worship

Encourager

Praising God is the remedy needed when you are feeling discourage and low in spirit. When you do feel discouraged, your flesh does not feel like praising God. Instead, praise and worship in times of feeling disappointed, isthe weapon you use to war against your flesh. Give praises to God instead of mourning and complaining. Your flesh with come in agreement with the praises you offer to God.

Scripture

Psalm 43:5
Why are you cast down, O my soul? And why are you disquieted within me? Hope in God; For I shall yet praise Him, The help of my countenance and my God.(NKJV)

Praise and Worship
Heart Notes

_____

_____

_____

_____

_____

_____

_____

_____

_____

_____

_____

_____

_____

Praise & Worship

Encourager

Sometimes we allow fear to make us prisoners. Fear of being rejected, sickness, needs not being met,understanding, uncertainty, or even fear of death. These emotions will cause feelings of depression and darkness. Fear can be conquered by allowing the Light of Jesus to shine on you and free you from your fears. When you begin to feel fearful, begin praising and worshipping God. Start with telling Him how much you love Him. Tell Him how you feel and how much you need Him to free you from fear. He is the Light that can overshadow any darkness.

Scripture

Psalm 27:1
The Lord is my light and my salvation whom shall I fear? (NKJV)

Praise & Worship
Heart Notes

_____

_____

_____

_____

_____

_____

_____

_____

_____

_____

_____

_____

_____

Setting Boundaries

Journey Ten

Setting Boundaries

Encourager

The bible commands us to control ourselves, whereas, our human nature desires to control others. If left unchecked, our natural desires dominate others. The development of your spiritual boundaries will help limit your selfish tendency to control and manipulate others. Likewise, boundaries also will protect you from those who have no self-control and who wish to control you. When you set clear and healthy boundaries, you are saying, "this is my jurisdiction and you have no right to interfere".

Scripture

Titus 2:12
And along with this gift comes the realization that God wants to turn from godless living and sinful pleasures and to live good, god-fearing lives day after day.

Setting Boundaries
Heart Notes

_____

_____

_____

_____

_____

_____

_____

_____

_____

_____

_____

_____

_____

Setting Boundaries

Encourager

Friends and love ones can have a great influence on youin very subtle ways. Many of the people in your lifemay not believe in the things of God; and often mock God. Your love for God equips you to guard against influences from others that are not wise. Wisdom is the result of allowing the Word to lead and guide your actions. It is the anchor needed to seal your commitment to God and draw others to Him. Therefore, the influence of the unbeliever does not affect your thoughts and attitudes. Therefore, you are the one doing the leading and have the greatest influence.

Scripture

Psalm 1:2
Blessed is the man Who walks not in the counsel of the ungodly, Nor stand in the path of sinners, Nor sit in the seat of the scornful; But his delight is in the law of the Lord and in His law He meditates day and night.(NKJV)

Setting Boundaries
Heart Notes

_____

_____

_____

_____

_____

_____

_____

_____

_____

_____

_____

_____

Setting Boundaries

Encourager

God's Word can be called "fences" in life. IT guards and protects you from the things that would cause destruction in your life. IT is a barrier to protect you from right or wrong, dos or don'ts, obedience or disobedience. It will set boundaries and protect you from all of the enemies of life.

Scripture

Psalm 61:3
For you has been a shelter for me, A strong tower from the enemy. (NKJV)

Setting Boundaries
Heart Notes

_____

_____

_____

_____

_____

_____

_____

_____

_____

_____

_____

_____

_____

Setting Boundaries

Encourager

When you stay in close relationship with God and follow God's Word, IT increases your knowledge and understanding. The more you read God's Word, the more you learn. Understanding of His Word becomes clearer and wisdom is gain.

Scripture

Proverbs 1:5
A wise man will hear and increase learning, And a man of understanding will attain wise counsel.
(NKJV)

Setting Boundaries
Heart Notes

_____

_____

_____

_____

_____

_____

_____

_____

_____

_____

_____

_____

_____

Setting Boundaries

Encourager

One of parent's greatest responsibilities is
teaching their children the Word of God. The
Word of God is the key to seeking wisdom. When
you teach your children God's Word, they learn
boundaries. They recognize when they stay in the
Word of God, there is safety. When they stray, the
Word of God will even bring them back in God's
boundaries, in due time.

Scripture

Proverbs 4:1-2
*Hear, my children, the instruction of a father, And
give attention to know understanding; For I give you
good doctrine: Do not forsake my law. (NKJV)*

Setting Boundaries
Heart Notes

_____

_____

_____

_____

_____

_____

_____

_____

_____

_____

_____

_____

_____

Expectations

Journey Eleven

Expectations

Encourager

Cheer up! You can have confidence knowing that you can depend on God. Expect and trust His promises.

Scripture

Psalm 31:24
Be of good courage, And He shall strengthen your heart, All you who hope in the Lord (NKJ).

Expectations
Heart Notes

_____

_____

_____

_____

_____

_____

_____

_____

_____

_____

_____

_____

_____

Expectations

Encourager

Being a student of the Word will bring out the best in your attitude. Reading scriptures is a witness to what God have done in the past. The more you know about what God has done, the more understanding and confidence you will have in what He is doing in the your life and the future. The Word admonishes that in all of your getting, get understanding. You can expect to receive the blessings promised, only when you understand.

Scripture

Romans 15:4
For whatever things were written before were written for our learning, that we through and comfort of the Scriptures might have hope. (NKJV)

Expectations
Heart Notes

_____

_____

_____

_____

_____

_____

_____

_____

_____

_____

_____

_____

_____

_____

Expectations

Encourager

Jeremiah knew from personal experience that God is faithful. God will test you through your trials, tribulations. He releases sufficient amount of hope needed for every test and trial. Hope, trust and have faith in God's promises. He is faithful!

Scripture

Lamentations 3:24
The Lord is my portion, says my soul, Therefore I hope in Him. (NKJV)

Expectations
Heart Notes

_____

_____

_____

_____

_____

_____

_____

_____

_____

_____

_____

_____

_____

_____

Expectations

Encourager

I pray that your heart will be flooded with God's Light, that you understand His Word and can see into your future. Knowing and understanding your spiritual inheritance that He has called you into, gives you the ability to walk into it.

Scripture

Ephesians 1:18
The eyes of your understanding being enlightened; that you may know what is the hope of His calling, what are the riches of the glory of His inheritance in the saints, (NKJV)

Expectations
Heart Notes

_____

_____

_____

_____

_____

_____

_____

_____

_____

_____

_____

_____

_____

Expectations

Encourager

Just as a farmer spend hours planting and plowing in his field. He does it expecting that eventually there will be a harvest. He has spent his time planting seeds, plowing, pulling up weed and watering his crop. He does this with hope, understanding and expectation for a future harvest. He realizes that this action is necessary and he expects a return. The same principle is needed in expecting God to do anything for you. What is it that you expect God to do for you? Have you planted the seeds necessary to receive your harvest?

Scripture

1 Corinthians 9:10
He that plows ought to be plowing in expectation; and he that threshes should be partaker of his expectation. (NKJV)

Expectations
Heart Notes

_____

_____

_____

_____

_____

_____

_____

_____

_____

_____

_____

_____

_____

_____

Balancing

Journey Twelve

Balancing

Encourager

Give glory to God knowing that by his mighty power at work in you. You are able to do far more than you would ever think, dream or even ask, above your highest petition of prayer, desires, thoughts and hopes.

Scripture

Ephesians 3:20
Now to Him who is able to do exceedingly, abundantly above all that we ask or think; according to the power that works in us. (NKJV)

Balancing
Heart Notes

_____

_____

_____

_____

_____

_____

_____

_____

_____

_____

_____

_____

_____

Balancing

Encourager

Paul spent many of his days in a physical prison, yet he remained spiritually free. You can too. When you understand your worth, value and your rich heritage, you will realize that all of God's blessings belong to you. It won't matter where you came from, what you are going through, or what you have done in the past, you can walk in confidence. Whether you are in a physical or spiritual prison, your freedom lies in knowing that God called and chose you to do His Will. Do it with love, dignity and honor.

Scripture

Ephesians 4:1-2
I therefore, the prisoner of the Lord, beseech you walk worthy of the calling with which you were called. (NKJV)

Balancing
Heart Notes

_____

_____

_____

_____

_____

_____

_____

_____

_____

_____

_____

_____

_____

Balancing

Encourager

How balance is your life? It is a good thing to sometimes take an evaluation of your life. Measuringhow balance you are, allows you to evaluate yourself. Are you involved in too many things? Do you need to prioritize certain things? Have you taken on too much? This is one of the traps that causes imbalance. Its okay to say no when asked to do something that you know you shouldn't. If you don't know what you should be doing, others will gladly tell you what they want you to do. Don't get caught up in dead works that take up a lot of your valuable time. Ask God to teach you to hear His voice. Put first things first in your life.

Scripture

John 9:4
I must do the work of Him who sent Me while it is day: the night is coming when no one can work.
(NKJV)

Balancing
Heart Notes

_____

_____

_____

_____

_____

_____

_____

_____

_____

_____

_____

_____

_____

Balancing

Encourager

As you continue putting the Word of God into practice, you will learn how to juggle all your roles. Adjusting the circumstances in your life without losing focus is the key in becoming balance. Practice makes perfect. You will become a pro, and won't be moved by people, things, or distractions that try to get your attention. Eventually, you will discern, lead and guided by the Holy Spirit and won't be moved by emotions or what appear to be your answers.

Scripture

Ephesians 4:14-16
That we should no longer be children tossed to and fro and carried about with every wind of doctrine, by the trickery of men, in the cunning craftiness of deceitful plotting. (NKJV)

Balancing
Heart Notes

_____

_____

_____

_____

_____

_____

_____

_____

_____

_____

_____

_____

_____

_____

Balancing

Encourager

Jesus Christ has given you His strength, His power, and His authority. Therefore you can do everything necessary to live your life with purpose and in abundance. There is nothing that is too challenging in your life that you are not equipped to have victory over.

Scripture

Philippians 4:13
I can do all things through Christ who strengthens me.
(NKJV)

Balancing
Heart Notes

Balancing

Encourager

Enter daily into the gates of the Lord with thanksgiving, and into His court with praises. Spend each day giving thanks to Him and bless the name of the Lord. Practice daily. Do your balancing **ACTS** in prayer. Balance your life everyday with adoration, confessions, thanksgiving and supplication. As you mature spiritually, you learn to bless the Lord!

Scripture

Psalms 100: 4
Enter His gates with thanksgiving And into His gates with praise, Be thankful to Him, and bless His name. (NKJV)

Balancing
Heart Notes

_____

_____

_____

_____

_____

_____

_____

_____

_____

_____

_____

_____

_____

Balancing

Encourager

God loves a cheerful giver. If you give, it will be given back to you. When you give Him your life; He returns whatever you give, good measure, pressed down, shaken together and running over. Hecauses people to give you from every direction. The Lord multiplies your giving with the same measure in which you give.

Scripture

Luke 6:38
Give and it shall be given to you: good measure, pressed down, shaken together, and running over will be put into your bosom. For the same measure that you use, it will be measured back to you. (NKJV)

Balancing
Heart Notes

_____

_____

_____

_____

_____

_____

_____

_____

_____

_____

_____

_____

_____

Balancing

Encourager

As you give your tithe and your offerings to the storehouse, God gives you the provisions you and your family need. He pours spiritual, physical and financial blessings in your life. Provisions include wisdom, favor and money. Sometimes all you need is one of the three.

Scripture

Malachi 3:10
Bring all the tithes into the storehouse That there may be food in My house, And try me now in this, Says the Lord of hosts, "If I will not open for you the windows of heaven And pour out for you such blessing that there will not be room enough to receive it.(NKJV)

Balancing
Heart Notes

_____

_____

_____

_____

_____

_____

_____

_____

_____

_____

_____

_____

_____

Balancing

Encourager

God, if you are please with me, please teach me your way. I want to know you and continue to find favor with you. I want to mirror or look like Him. Can you see Him in yourself?

Scripture

Exodus 33:13
 Show me now Your way, that I may know you."(NKJV)

Balancing
Heart Notes

_____

_____

_____

_____

_____

_____

_____

_____

_____

_____

_____

_____

_____

Balancing

Encourager

The same power that raised Jesus from the dead lives on the inside of you. Saying that is one thing, but the power lies in believing, experiencing and operating in it. Knowing Him in His Power is having the ability to operate in boldness and victory. It is being confident enough in what He has called you to be and produce the changes the world need. No matter what problems and issues people in this world face, you are equipped and empowered to bring back to life any and everything that is dead.

Scripture

Philippians 3:10
That I may know Him, and the power of His resurrection, and the fellowship of His sufferings, being made conformable unto His death. (NKJV)

Balancing
Heart Notes

_____

_____

_____

_____

_____

_____

_____

_____

_____

_____

_____

_____

_____

Confessions

A confession is not asking God for what you want. He has already given you whatever you need. It is up to you to exercisewhat He gave you. He delegated and gave you the authority, and power to speak, declare, and decree for whatever His Will is for your life.
Read and study the Word, therefore, you will know what to pray and confess.

Confessions

I am the righteousness of God created in Jesus.
HIS spirit lives in me.

Jesus has given me the keys to the Kingdom. I have the power to bind and loose on earth and whatever I bind and lose on earth, it will be done in the heavens or the spirit realm.

I have the authority to speak the Word of God and it shall be established.

I am the redeemed of the Lord.

I believe what the Word of God says.

I can do what I Word of God says

I am what the Word of God says I am.

I do not focus on negative things seen, but my focus is on spiritual things that are unseen.

God has anointed me as a king.
As a king, I rule and reign.

I now choose to walk in my authority, dominion and power.

I am now ready for the awaiting harvest.

The harvest is plenteous, but the laborers are few.

I am a laborer of the harvest

I am blessed and highly favored.

My mind has been renewed and transformed to the mind of Christ.

I think Kingdom.

I am Kingdom minded.

I walk kingdom,

I am kingdom.

I am ready to give birth to my purpose!

In Jesus Name!

Journaling

"To Know Him"
Heart Notes

_____

_____

_____

_____

_____

_____

_____

_____

_____

_____

_____

_____

Journaling

"To Know Him"
Heart Notes

_____

_____

_____

_____

_____

_____

_____

_____

_____

_____

_____

_____

_____

Journaling

"To Know Him"
Heart Notes

_____

_____

_____

_____

_____

_____

_____

_____

_____

_____

_____

_____

Journaling

"To Know Him"
Heart Notes

_____

_____

_____

_____

_____

_____

_____

_____

_____

_____

_____

_____

Journaling

"To Know Him"
Heart Notes

ABOUT THE WRITER

*Cheryl Swinton-Weston*greatest fulfillment is when God uses her to speak hope, truth and life into the heart of someone else. Her love, compassion and passion for others is the result of her surrendering and allowing God to process her through life's pain, struggles and issues. She demonstrates her mission by transforming her life experiences through mentoring, coaching, preaching, teaching, writing and publishing.

Cheryl has earned a Master of Science in Human Service and an Associate Degree in Early Childhood Education. She has certification in National Accreditation of Phlebotomy and NTA Professional Life Coaching. She has also earned her Itinerant Deacon Ordination by the A.M.E. Church and Grace Cathedral Ministries Fellowship. Cheryl is founder and CEO of Grace Us Living Publication and Special Nest Village, a retreat and restoration home for professional women.

She is a native of Mount Pleasant SC; and currently resides in Greenville SC. Her most quoted scripture is Proverbs 3:5-6. She strongly believes that our steps are ordered by God. Therefore, many of our journeys are testimonies of God's love, hope, redemption and restoration power.

Cheryl is an expert in helping other's shine and believes every person have at least one story to share with the world!

"To Know Him"
Planner

Date: _____

1. _____

2. _____

3 _____

4. _____

5 _____

6. _____

7. _____

8. _____

9. _____

10. _____

11. _____

12. _____

13. _____

14. _____

"To Know Him"
Planner

Date:_____

1._____

2._____

3_____

4._____

5_____

6._____

7._____

8._____

9._____

10._____

11._____

12._____

13._____

14._____

"To Know Him"
Planner

Date: _____

1. _____
2. _____
3 _____
4. _____
5 _____
6. _____
7. _____
8. _____
9. _____
10. _____
11. _____
12. _____
13. _____
14. _____

"To Know Him"
Planner

Date:_____

1._____

2._____

3_____

4._____

5_____

6._____

7._____

8._____

9._____

10._____

11._____

12._____

13._____

14._____

"To Know Him"
Planner

Date:_____

1._____

2._____

3_____

4._____

5_____

6._____

7._____

8._____

9._____

10._____

11._____

12._____

13._____

14._____

References

The New King James Version Bible

The King James Version Bible

The New International Version

The Life Application Bible

The Living Bible

For more information about the ministry of Cheryl Swinton-Weston and a list of available books, small group studies, publications, speaking engagement, workshops and CD messages, you may email, twitter, and Facebook, call or write:

Grace Us Living Publications (GULP)
Email:graceusliving@yahoo.com
Website: www.graceusliving.com
Phone: 843-406-3499

Publications and books are available on amazon.com and www.graceusliving.com.

www.ingramcontent.com/pod-product-compliance
Lightning Source LLC
Chambersburg PA
CBHW061823040426
42447CB00012B/2780